P9-EET-867

FRONTLINE
HEROES

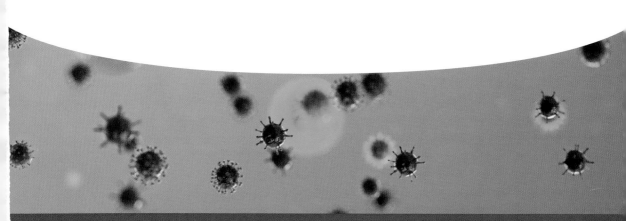

BY EMILY HUDD

CONTENT CONSULTANT
Mark N. Lurie, PhD
Associate Professor of Epidemiology, International Health Institute
Brown University School of Public Health

Cover image: Health-care workers and other frontline heroes wore
special protective gear during the COVID-19 pandemic.

Core Library

An Imprint of Abdo Publishing
abdobooks.com

abdobooks.com

Published by Abdo Publishing, a division of ABDO, PO Box 398166, Minneapolis, Minnesota 55439. Copyright © 2021 by Abdo Consulting Group, Inc. International copyrights reserved in all countries. No part of this book may be reproduced in any form without written permission from the publisher. Core Library™ is a trademark and logo of Abdo Publishing.

Printed in the United States of America, North Mankato, Minnesota
062020
092020

Cover Photo: Frederic Dides/SIPA/Shutterstock Images
Interior Photos: Ozge Elif Kizil/Anadolu Agency/Getty Images, 4–5; iStockphoto, 8, 30, 43; Chinatopix/AP Images, 10; Red Line Editorial, 12, 37; Charlie Riedel/AP Images, 16–17, 18; Hannah McKay/PA Wire/URN:53780375/Press Association/AP Images, 21; Gerald Herbert/AP Images, 24; Shutterstock Images, 26–27; Takayuki Hamai/The Yomiuri Shimbun/AP Images, 32, 45; Aitana Fotografia/Shutterstock Images, 34–35; Ted S. Warren/AP Images, 39

Editor: Charly Haley
Series Designer: Jake Nordby

Library of Congress Control Number: 2020936516

Publisher's Cataloging-in-Publication Data

Names: Hudd, Emily, author.
Title: Frontline heroes / by Emily Hudd
Description: Minneapolis, Minnesota : Abdo Publishing, 2021 | Series: Core library guide to COVID-19 | Includes online resources and index
Identifiers: ISBN 9781532194054 (lib. bdg.) | ISBN 9781644945025 (pbk.) | ISBN 9781098212964 (ebook)
Subjects: LCSH: Medical personnel--Juvenile literature. | Food service employees--Juvenile literature. | School employees--Juvenile literature. | Volunteers--Juvenile literature. | Heroes--Juvenile literature. | Epidemics--Juvenile literature. | COVID-19 (Disease)--Juvenile literature.
Classification: DDC 610.69--dc23

CONTENTS

CHAPTER ONE

ON THE FRONT LINES

Doors burst open on the back of an ambulance. Paramedics roll a patient lying on a stretcher into the hospital. Alarms ring out. The hospital hallway is packed. Curtains separate each patient. Doctors and nurses wear protective gear from head to toe. Goggles and clear, plastic shields cover their faces. White and blue papery full-body suits loosely cover the rest of them. Some have gloves taped to their sleeves. The paramedics look for an open place to put their patient.

Emergency medical workers pull a COVID-19 patient out of an ambulance and into a hospital.

Finally they find a spot. As soon as the stretcher stops rolling, a nurse arrives. She gets details on the new patient. The man had a fever and was having trouble breathing. He was infected with COVID-19.

Meanwhile a doctor catches her breath between seeing patients. She is overwhelmed by the number of people coming in with fevers and difficulty breathing. To her, fighting COVID-19 feels like war. But the enemy is spreading quickly and invisibly through the air. Health-care workers like her fight on the front lines by going to work. First responders and food service workers are also on the front lines helping people. Others help win the war by slowing the spread and staying at home. People make sacrifices, big and small.

WHAT IS COVID-19?

COVID-19 is a disease caused by a virus called SARS-CoV-2. This virus was discovered in late 2019. An outbreak of COVID-19 began at that time. People all over the world became sick, and there was no cure.

SARS-CoV-2 is a type of virus known as a coronavirus. Coronaviruses cause respiratory problems, such as having trouble breathing. COVID-19 symptoms include shortness of breath and fever. Some people have very mild symptoms or no symptoms at all. For others, the disease seems similar to having the flu. They are only sick for a week or two. But COVID-19 can also be deadly. People who are most at risk

PERSPECTIVES

THE WORST DAY YET

During the pandemic, Julie Eason worked as a respiratory therapist at a hospital in Brooklyn, New York City. The hospital was one of three in New York City set aside for COVID-19 patients. Extra beds for patients were put in the cafeteria. In an April 2020 interview, Eason gave advice to hospital workers around the country. She said, "Get ready, because whatever you've imagined as your worst day ever, you've not seen it yet. We normally have a couple patients that are this level sick. [Now] our ICUs are filled with them, filled with them, and none of them can breathe."

COMMON COVID-19 SYMPTOMS

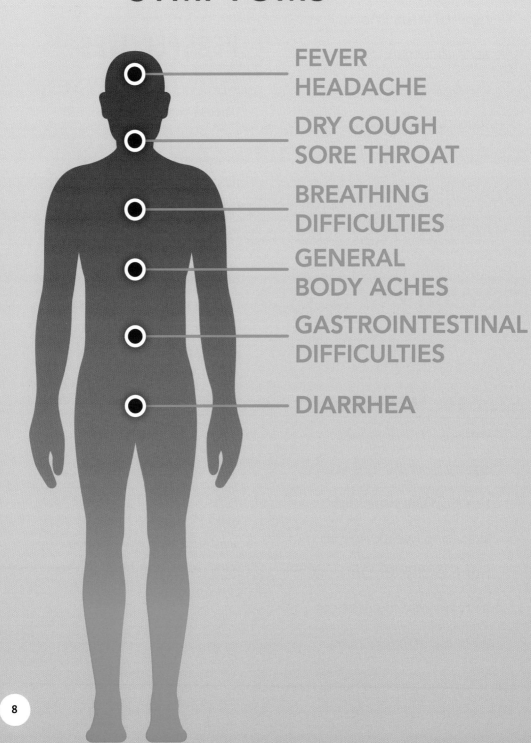

FEVER
HEADACHE

DRY COUGH
SORE THROAT

BREATHING
DIFFICULTIES

GENERAL
BODY ACHES

GASTROINTESTINAL
DIFFICULTIES

DIARRHEA

are adults older than 65 and people with underlying health issues. An underlying health issue affects how someone's body fights against illnesses. People who already have lung and heart issues are especially at risk for severe COVID-19 symptoms.

Scientists discovered that COVID-19 spreads easily from close human contact. When people cough, sneeze, and talk, the virus can spread through the air in tiny droplets. It can enter the eyes, noses, or mouths of people close by. They become infected.

HOW DID THE OUTBREAK START?

COVID-19 was first seen in Wuhan, China. It spread rapidly through Wuhan, then other parts of China, then the rest of the world. At first, people did not know how to slow the spread. Some weren't concerned because they didn't know how dangerous the disease was. Some people had the disease but didn't have symptoms, so they accidentally spread it to others. Italy, Iran, South

Mild COVID-19 symptoms include fever and cough, while more severe symptoms include breathing difficulties.

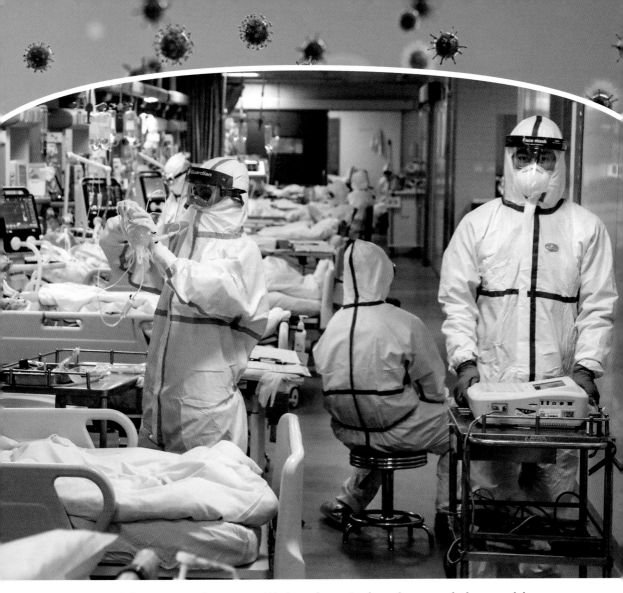

Health-care workers at a Wuhan hospital and around the world wore special clothing to protect themselves from COVID-19.

Korea, and Spain were hit hard early in the outbreak. On March 11, 2020, the World Health Organization (WHO) declared COVID-19 a pandemic. A pandemic is a disease that has spread worldwide. At that time, more than 118,000 cases had been reported in more than 100 countries.

On March 26, the United States became the country with the most cases. It had 82,404 cases that day. The country with the second-most was China at 81,782. Health officials and government leaders around the world tried to slow the spread. They encouraged social distancing. They told people to avoid leaving home and gathering in large groups. Health officials warned that for people at high risk of severe symptoms, gatherings should be kept to ten people or fewer. Businesses such as restaurants began closing. People worked at home to stay safe. But not everyone had the option to stay home. Frontline heroes continued going to work.

STILL WORKING

For some people, shutting down businesses is not a big problem. They may have savings or high-paying jobs. They may be able to work from home. But many people

US WORKERS ON THE FRONT LINES

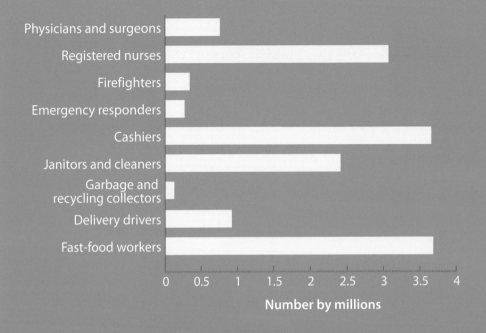

Number by millions

This graph shows the number of frontline workers in 2018, the most recent data available from the US Bureau of Labor Statistics when the COVID-19 pandemic began. What are the benefits to having many people working on the front lines during a crisis? What are some drawbacks?

are not in those situations. People with little money can't afford to stop working. During the pandemic, some had to put themselves at risk to pay their bills and support their families. Grocery stores and other places with low-paid workers stayed open, and many of their workers could not afford to quit.

A March 2020 US study looked at which kinds of workers come into contact with the most people. It also looked at how much each job pays. Results showed health-care workers were at high risk. They are well-trained for dealing with diseases, but their work is still stressful. They work directly with sick people. Some, such as doctors, make lots of money. But others receive lower pay.

Many other high-risk jobs pay low wages. Cashiers and delivery drivers were suddenly on the front lines as well. These essential workers helped make sure people had food and other supplies. But some felt they had to risk their lives at work because they needed their next paychecks.

Staying at home helps slow the spread of COVID-19 because it limits contact between people. Office jobs and computer work can be done from home.

But people in frontline jobs went to work and saw many other people. They risked getting coughed or sneezed on by customers or patients.

Rather than feeling like heroes, some frontline workers felt trapped or scared. Still, these workers bravely served others. Whether in a hospital, a grocery store, or elsewhere, frontline heroes helped people around the world during the pandemic.

MAKING A DIFFERENCE

New Jersey doctor Frank Gabrin's coworkers knew him as a positive person. He encouraged younger doctors to stick with their career when it got tough. He believed it was rewarding to care for others. He said health-care workers made a difference for people by helping them get better, one patient at a time. Gabrin died on March 31, 2020, because of COVID-19. He was 60 years old. He was the first US doctor to die from the disease.

STRAIGHT TO THE
SOURCE

Volunteer emergency responder Mat Giachetti helped COVID-19 patients in New Jersey. He said:

> *We've never seen anything like this before. We're scared. But we're still going out there. . . . We'll always go in with masks and gloves. But when we [have a coronavirus case], we're putting gowns on. We're putting goggles on. We're duct-taping the sleeves where our first pair of gloves are on. If you don't do every step, there's a chance for exposure. . . .*
>
> *There's something ingrained in us to help. I don't think that makes us any more heroic than a doctor or a nurse. There's really no difference in your mindset whether you're paid to do this or you're a volunteer. . . . It's the need to help your fellow man that keeps us going.*

Source: Keith Sargeant. "EMS Squads on the Front Lines of the Coronavirus Crisis: 'We're Scared. But We're Still Going Out There.'" *NJ Advance Media*, 6 Apr. 2020, nj.com. Accessed 22 Apr. 2020.

WHAT'S THE BIG IDEA?

Read the primary source text carefully and determine its main idea. Explain how the main idea is supported by details, naming two or three of those supporting details.

HEALTH-CARE WORKERS

People who choose a health-care career know they are not going to have it easy. Not only is their schooling difficult, but their jobs carry many risks. Despite training for life and death situations, many are still scared sometimes. Health-care workers were on the true front lines of the pandemic. They worked in hospitals full of infected people. They stood by dying people's bedsides. They helped people recover too. They were heroes because

A doctor at a Kansas hospital cleans the face shield that he wears to see COVID-19 patients.

Some places offered drive-up COVID-19 tests to protect health-care workers and others from being exposed to patients.

they bravely continued working. They used their skills for the good of others.

During the pandemic, health-care workers focused on helping people with severe COVID-19 symptoms. These workers tested people for COVID-19 too. The test involved putting long cotton swabs up a person's nose for 15 seconds. Then the swabs were tested in a lab to see if they showed the virus.

CHANGES FOR SAFETY

The pandemic changed how hospitals and care centers worked. New dress codes and cleaning procedures were a few of many changes. US health-care buildings relied on the US Centers for Disease Control and Prevention (CDC) and the Food and Drug Administration (FDA) for the safest guidelines to follow.

Nursing home staff had to be extra careful

PERSPECTIVES

CHILDBIRTH DURING THE PANDEMIC

American nurse Chandler Scott helped deliver babies during the COVID-19 pandemic. She explained how the birthing process at her Georgia hospital had changed because of the pandemic. Everyone had to wear gowns, masks, and full-body protective gear. After birth, she said, "Babies get separated immediately from parents and placed in quarantine until deemed safe to return to the mother." Parents got limited time with newborns. Sometimes nurses even set up video streaming so parents could look at their baby while they were separated.

during the pandemic. They worked with people who were at the highest risk of becoming seriously ill from COVID-19. In early 2020, the CDC restricted guest visits at nursing homes. It also stopped group events and group dining. Volunteers or nonessential people such as hair stylists were no longer allowed into nursing homes. But sometimes these changes were not enough.

Some places still had tragic losses. A nursing home in Michigan saw several employees and nearly half of its residents get infected. Its employees did all they could to be careful. They wore protective gear and masks. They took their temperatures before starting each shift. Any employee with a fever was sent home.

NOT ENOUGH NURSES

A study done in the 2010s found that many nurses worked 12-hour shifts. Long shifts meant they only had to work three days a week. But the study also found that nurses often worked overtime. They had to stay late or work extra days when coworkers couldn't come in or when there was an overflow of patients. Even before

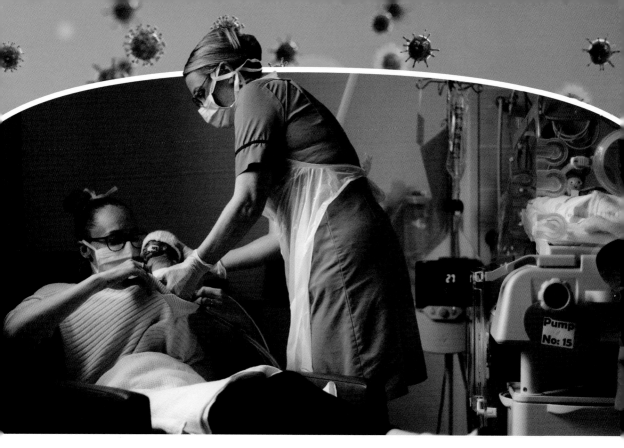

A nurse checks on a new mother and her baby in the United Kingdom during the pandemic.

the pandemic, nurses regularly faced challenging, exhausting days.

During the pandemic, some nurses had to be away from home for 16 to 17 hours a day up to seven days a week. Nurses worked extra hours, but some hospitals still did not have enough staff to care for everyone. By mid-March, governments asked retired nurses and other health-care professionals to go back to work.

MEDICAL RESEARCHERS

Medical researchers played a key role in fighting COVID-19. They worked in labs and were indirectly on the front lines while trying to create a treatment or vaccine. Vaccines help prevent people from getting a disease. By April 2020, researchers had made progress studying COVID-19. But it takes a long time to develop a vaccine and to produce enough doses to release it to the public.

They desperately needed workers.

Many patients needed treatment for COVID-19. But other people still needed help with other health problems. Health-care workers also continued to care for those with broken bones, heart attacks, cancer, and other conditions. These patients were all kept separate from those with COVID-19 to avoid spreading the virus.

PUTTING LOVED ONES AT RISK

Italian doctor Cecilia Bartalena changed her way of life at home and at work because of COVID-19. She slept, ate, and washed in different rooms than her daughter and husband. At the hospital, she stayed away from patients when possible to be safe. People called her a hero, but she didn't feel like one. She was afraid of spreading the disease. But she continued working for the greater good.

American doctor Tim Cheng similarly decided to separate himself from family members. For a few nights, he slept in his car and in spare rooms at the hospital. Then his wife thought of the idea to pitch a tent in their garage. He chose to eat, sleep, and live in the tent in order to protect his family.

MENTAL HEALTH AND STRESS

Besides physical dangers, working in health care during the pandemic took a toll mentally. In 2020, researchers studied more than 1,200 health-care workers from 34 hospitals in China. They found that mental health conditions were made worse by the pandemic. The workers were directly involved with caring for COVID-19 patients. They were 50 percent more likely to

Health-care workers celebrate outside their hospital as the New Orleans (Louisiana) Jazz Orchestra plays music for them at a distance. Many organizations tried to support health-care workers and boost their mental health.

experience depression, anxiety, and distress than other health-care workers. Many workers were overwhelmed by their workload and concerned for their personal health. These factors affected their mental health.

British nurse Joanne Morrell felt frustrated when people didn't take social distancing seriously. People who kept going out angered her. In a TV interview, Morrell asked people to please follow safety suggestions. These steps would help people keep themselves safe. They would also show respect for nurses and other health-care workers on the front lines.

STRAIGHT TO THE
SOURCE

Sara Wazlavek worked as a nurse at a Georgia hospital during the pandemic. Many people felt nurses were heroic in their work. But for Wazlavek it was just the right thing to do.

I've never seen anything like this before. . . . No one wants to put their family's lives on the line. I come home with the knowledge that I might be bringing COVID into my home, that it could kill me, my husband, or my kids. I didn't think becoming a nurse would mean possibly losing my family, or that I would be the cause.

Not everyone can do this job. It takes training. If everyone who was afraid quit, who would be left? What makes me so special that I can stay home when others are putting their lives at risk? . . . I want to help the people in our community who need us.

Source: David Blank. "World Health Day Honors Nurses on the Front Lines. Meet the Heroes Dealing with Coronavirus." *CNN*, 7 Apr. 2020, cnn.com. Accessed 23 Apr. 2020.

BACK IT UP

The speaker in this passage is using evidence to support a point. Write a paragraph describing the point being made. Then write down two or three pieces of evidence used to make the point.

ESSENTIAL SERVICE WORKERS

By the end of March 2020, nearly half the US population was under shelter-in-place orders, also called stay-at-home orders. The orders were issued by state governments. They meant people had to stay at home all the time and only go out for necessary reasons such as getting groceries. Only essential businesses could stay open. But deciding what was essential was complicated.

Mail, banking, food, medical, and home and auto repair businesses were considered

During the pandemic, people with no symptoms still wore face masks to reduce their risk of spreading the virus.

essential. Sports venues, gyms, movie theaters, and malls were nonessential. Service workers were needed to keep businesses going. They risked contact with many people even when they followed safety guidelines. Health officials recommended that people in public stay 6 feet (1.8 m) apart. But this is tough to do for some kinds of workers.

RESTAURANT AND DELIVERY WORKERS

Restaurant and delivery jobs may have seemed ordinary in 2019. But after the pandemic started, these jobs became important and sometimes dangerous. Restaurants were forced to close dining areas due to social distancing guidelines. But they could provide food with to-go orders or in drive-throughs. Scientists found that the virus was unlikely to be spread on food.

Restaurant workers had uncertain futures because they did not know if their companies would make enough money to stay open. Additionally, they often prepared food in close quarters with other workers. They interacted with many customers too.

Delivery orders rose when people began staying at home more. Delivery drivers risked being in contact with people and spreading COVID-19. Businesses started offering contactless delivery. This meant employees did not come in contact with customers. Some stores allowed online order and pick up. A person could drive to the store but stay in the

PERSPECTIVES

LUCKY OR UNSAFE?

Kelsey Taylor was a fast-food worker in Seattle, Washington, in early 2020. When the pandemic hit, she became an essential worker. She made food for drive-through and delivery. Sometimes she felt lucky that she could still work and receive paychecks. Other times she worried she would get sick. She said, "Every day, I wake up torn between being grateful that I still have a job and being terrified for my own safety. . . . My job is willing to let me take the time off, but, like a majority of other food service people, I have no paid time off . . . so I keep working."

Truck drivers were on the front lines as they made sure stores stayed stocked with the supplies people needed.

car. An employee would bring out the items and place them in the car.

Some customers may have been staying home because they had COVID-19. Some delivery drivers said they were not getting paid enough for the risk they were taking. They decided the best way to get attention, help, and protection was to go on strike.

GROCERY CLERKS AND GAS STATION WORKERS

As restaurants closed, people began preparing more food at home. Grocery stores saw increased sales. Stores hired more people to respond to this demand.

They also needed to replace employees who had stopped working to stay home. Additionally, grocery stores changed the way they operated. Some limited the number of people allowed inside. Many put up clear shields between cashiers and customers.

Despite these changes, grocery store employees were at risk. They saw hundreds of people a day. Sometimes they didn't have enough supplies, such as gloves and masks. To make matters worse, grocery store workers are often paid low wages. Some

AMAZON WORKERS STRIKE

Employees at an Amazon delivery facility in New York worried about going to work. The building had more than 5,000 employees. Several had tested positive for the virus. One manager, Chris Smalls, worried the building wasn't being cleaned enough. He decided to help plan a walkout for workers. But not working has consequences. Smalls said Amazon doesn't pay people when they choose to stay home and be safe with their families. In late March 2020, more than 100 workers at an Amazon delivery station in Italy went on strike.

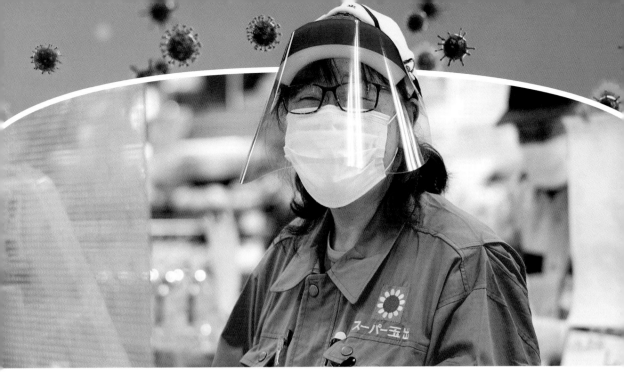

A grocery store worker in Japan wears a mask and face shield during the pandemic.

felt they were in danger because of COVID-19, but they continued to work because they needed the money.

Karleigh Frisbie Brogan was a grocery store worker who felt overwhelmed during the pandemic. Before the pandemic, she thought work was enjoyable and easygoing. Once COVID-19 spread and caused business closures, she realized she was on the front lines. Panicked people flooded the store each day. Some thanked her for her bravery and service, as if she had served in the military. Brogan worried every day about getting COVID-19 from a shopper. But she decided to continue to work as long as she was healthy.

A gas station in Tennessee switched to full service during the pandemic. At full service stations, workers pump people's gas for them. Customers drive their car up and stay inside. This type of service limits the number of people touching gas station pumps. Many workers still worried about getting sick. But people showed up for essential service jobs to help keep their communities running.

EXPLORE ONLINE

Chapter Three talks about essential service workers. Explore this website about jobs on the front lines. Which are most at risk? How does that compare to how much the jobs pay? Compare and contrast the information there with information from this chapter about job safety during the COVID-19 pandemic. What new information did you learn from the website?

THE WORKERS WHO FACE THE GREATEST CORONAVIRUS RISK

abdocorelibrary.com/frontline-heroes

OTHER COMMUNITY WORKERS

Many essential workers are needed to keep communities running smoothly. These workers include janitors, police officers, and others. They may not face the risk of interacting with as many people each day as health-care and service workers do. But they still play an important role on the front lines.

Janitors and building managers were on the front lines of cleaning. They provided hand sanitizer to people in their buildings.

Janitors helped slow the spread of COVID-19 by keeping buildings clean.

They washed doorknobs and other frequently touched surfaces. The COVID-19 virus can live on surfaces, but soap and other cleaning products kill it.

Government leaders were on the front lines of the fight against COVID-19 too. They made rules to keep people safe. This included shelter-in-place orders. These leaders had to stay updated with information and recommendations from the WHO, the CDC, and medical professionals. Government leaders also made aid available to struggling businesses and people who were suddenly unemployed.

Schools closed to follow social distancing guidelines, so the need for daycare services increased. Daycare workers were important because essential workers still needed people to watch their children. In Arkansas, one woman knew how hard it could be to find child care during a sudden crisis, so she decided to help out. She formerly worked in child care, so she agreed to babysit a health-care worker's kids.

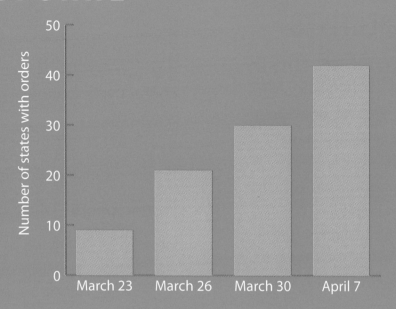

SHELTER-IN-PLACE ORDERS BY STATE

As the pandemic continued, more and more government leaders issued statewide shelter-in-place orders. Do you think all states should have the same orders and guidelines, or do you think each state should decide what to do for itself? Explain your answer.

FIRST RESPONDERS

First responders keep people safe and help in emergencies. They include ambulance workers, firefighters, and police officers. They are trained for responding to crises, but that doesn't make working during a pandemic easier. They were still at risk of

PERSPECTIVES

NEW YORK HIT HARD

As COVID-19 spread through the United States, New York became the state with the most cases. New York City alone had more than 205,000 cases and more than 17,200 deaths by mid-June. Officers working in the New York City Police Department (NYPD) were among those affected. More than 40 NYPD officers died from COVID-19. Police Chief Martin Morales said, "COVID hit us hard and the numbers were going up." On April 9, nearly 20 percent of officers called in sick. That was more than 7,000 workers. But by May 7, 91 percent of infected cops had recovered. More than 4,800 had returned to work.

getting or spreading COVID-19 because they came in close contact with people.

Emergency medical services (EMS) include people who work in ambulances or respond to 911 calls. They bring people in need to hospitals for medical care. Their work is stressful and fast-paced every day.

Firefighters are always frontline heroes. They rush into dangerous situations and risk their lives

Although firefighters always wear special gear to protect themselves from fires, many started wearing gear to protect themselves from COVID-19 too.

fighting fires. But during the pandemic, they had an added risk of disease. Some firefighters got infected with COVID-19. On April 8, 2020, the first Chicago, Illinois, firefighter died of the disease.

Police aim to respond quickly and serve the community at all times. During the pandemic, they helped in many ways. Sometimes helping meant quarantining police officers who showed symptoms.

THE FUTURE OF HEALTH-CARE TECHNOLOGY

Many businesses relied on technology to stay connected during the pandemic, including the health-care industry. Telemedicine is when patients get medical care by phone, video, or an app. It has been used in rural areas for years, but it boomed in 2020. It was helpful when hospitals focused on COVID-19 patients. People could stay home and still talk to a doctor or nurse about other health problems. They could show or tell symptoms, get diagnosed, and even get a prescription. Telemedicine was so helpful that some experts anticipated it would remain popular after the pandemic ended.

Other times it was enforcing shelter-in-place laws. In March, French police officers could fine people more than $140 for going outside without an essential reason. Some people thought fines for leaving home were harsh. Others believed it was a good way to stop the spread of COVID-19.

People who continued going to work during the COVID-19 pandemic risked their lives for others. Health-care workers helped people sickened by the disease. Cashiers and delivery drivers helped people get supplies and food to stay home. First responders answered calls for COVID-19 and for other emergencies. Daycare workers took care of children so people could keep working. No matter the risk or reason, many frontline heroes were recognized for their hard work.

FURTHER EVIDENCE

Chapter Four talks about community workers and government leaders who made shelter-in-place orders. Identify the main point and some key supporting evidence. Look at this website. Find a quote that supports the chapter's main point. Does the quote support a piece of evidence already in the chapter? Or does it add a new piece of information?

SEE WHICH STATES AND CITIES TOLD RESIDENTS TO STAY HOME

abdocorelibrary.com/frontline-heroes

FAST FACTS

- COVID-19 is a disease caused by a virus called SARS-CoV-2. SARS-CoV-2 is a type of virus known as a coronavirus. Coronaviruses cause respiratory problems such as having trouble breathing. Scientists discovered COVID-19 spreads through close human contact.

- Some people started working from home to slow the spread of the virus. Others had to keep going in to work. Some did not feel they had a choice. They depended on their paychecks in order to support their families.

- Health-care workers are trained to work during a crisis, but COVID-19 put overwhelming stress on them mentally and physically. They worked long hours and had busy shifts. Some places faced a shortage of nurses.

- Health-care workers risked their own lives and the lives of loved ones. To avoid spreading the disease at home, some decided to quarantine themselves.

- Shelter-in-place orders listed post offices, banks, restaurants, grocery stores, hospitals and clinics, and home and auto repair businesses as essential. Sports venues, gyms, movie theaters, and malls were nonessential.

- People working for fast-food restaurants, delivery businesses, grocery stores, and gas stations found themselves on the front lines of the pandemic. These jobs are often not highly paid. Many businesses put new procedures in place to reduce contact between employees and customers, but some employees felt they were being asked to work without enough resources.

- Janitors and building managers were on the front lines of cleaning and taking care of buildings and the people who lived or worked there.

- Daycare workers, government leaders, and first responders made it possible for people to keep working as safely as possible. Daycare workers watched children of other frontline workers. Government leaders made laws, and first responders acted quickly in emergencies.

STOP AND
THINK

Tell the Tale

Chapter Three of this book discusses essential workers on the front lines of the COVID-19 pandemic. Imagine you are a delivery driver or restaurant worker. Write 200 words about what you see, hear, and do. How could you stay safe while helping others?

Surprise Me

Chapter One describes what COVID-19 is and how the pandemic started. After reading this book, what two or three facts about infectious diseases did you find most surprising? Write a few sentences about each fact. Why did you find each fact surprising?

Dig Deeper

After reading this book, what questions do you still have about frontline workers during the COVID-19 pandemic? With an adult's help, find a few reliable sources that can help you answer your questions. Write a paragraph about what you learned.

Say What?

Studying diseases can mean learning a lot of new vocabulary. Find five words in this book you've never heard before. Use a dictionary to find out what they mean. Then write the meanings in your own words, and use each word in a new sentence.

GLOSSARY

essential
needed or necessary

exposure
the act of being unprotected from or coming into contact with something

ICUs
intensive care units, located in hospitals

ingrained
being a deep belief or attitude

prescription
medication given by a doctor

quarantine
a separated space from others or the act of separating oneself from others to avoid spreading a disease

respiratory
having to do with the lungs and airways

social distancing
also referred to as physical distancing, the act of staying away from others

strike
a walkout or refusal to work

ONLINE RESOURCES

To learn more about frontline heroes during the COVID-19 pandemic, visit our free resource websites below.

Visit **abdocorelibrary.com** or scan this QR code for free Common Core resources for teachers and students, including vetted activities, multimedia, and booklinks, for deeper subject comprehension.

Visit **abdobooklinks.com** or scan this QR code for free additional online weblinks for further learning. These links are routinely monitored and updated to provide the most current information available.

LEARN MORE

Alkire, Jessie. *Medicine: From Hippocrates to Jonas Salk*. Abdo Publishing, 2019.

Huddleston, Emma. *Work in the Health Care Industry*. ReferencePoint Press, 2020.

INDEX

About the Author

Emily Hudd lives in Minnesota with her husband. She enjoys writing books for students. When she isn't writing, she is often reading or staying active.